SPORTS ON THE EDGE!

EXTREME SKY SURFING

TAMRA B. ORR

Cavendish Square

New York

Published in 2014 by Cavendish Square Publishing, LLC
303 Park Avenue South, Suite 1247, New York, NY 10010

First Edition

Website: cavendishsq.com

CPSIA Compliance Information: Batch #WS13CSQ

All websites were available and accurate when this book was sent to press.

LIBRARY OF CONGRESS CATALOGING-IN-PUBLICATION DATA
Orr, Tamra.
Extreme skysurfing / Tamra B. Orr.
p. cm. — (Sports on the edge!)
Includes bibliographical references and index.
Summary: "Explores the sport of extreme skysurfing."—Provided by publisher.
ISBN 978-1-60870-232-9 (hardcover) ISBN 978-1-62712-136-1 (paperback)
ISBN 978-1-60870-865-9 (ebook)
1. Skysurfing—Juvenile literature. 2. Extreme sports—Juvenile literature. I. Title.
GV770.23O77 2013
797.56—dc23
2011034668

EDITOR: Christine Florie
ART DIRECTOR: Anahid Hamparian   SERIES DESIGNER: Kristen Branch

EXPERT READER: W. Scott "Douva" Lewis, U.S. bronze medalist skysurfer

Photo research by Marybeth Kavanagh

Cover photo by Jump Run Productions/Image Bank/Getty Images
The photographs in this book are used by permission and through the courtesy of: *Getty Images*: Jump Run Productions/Image Bank, 1, 2-3; *The Image Works*: Actionplus/ TopFoto, 4, 5, 12, 13, 17, 23, 31, 32, back cover; *Alamy*: Buzz Pictures, 7; StockShot, 10, 34, back cover; PhotoStock-Israel, 24; blickwinkel, 30, 38, back cover; *Newscom*: Andrey Veselov/AFP/Getty Images, 8; Michel Pissotte/DPPI/Icon SMI, 11, 27(top), 29, back cover; *AP Photo*: SECTOR NO LIMITS TEAM-HO, 15; Bruno Brokken, 21; *SuperStock*: Photri Images, 20, back cover; Flirt, 37; *Corbis*: Benelux, 27(bottom)

Printed in the United States of America

Contents

ONE
SURFING THE SKY

YOU SIT IN the airplane and look out the window at the bright blue sky and thick white clouds passing by. You hear the engine rumbling somewhere close, and the only thing louder is the sound of your heart beating quickly. Suddenly, the light mounted next to the plane's exit turns red. It's time to open the plane's door. In just a moment, the red light will turn to green, and you will leap out into the sky.

A SKYSURFER BEGINS HIS DESCENT, WHICH USUALLY INVOLVES FLIPS, TURNS, AND TWISTS.

Before the light turns green, however, you do your third gear check. In the first check, which was done before you even put your gear on, you made sure your equipment was in good shape and nothing was missing. Next, once you had all of your gear on, you adjusted the **harness** straps and double-checked that every part of the rig was secure. The reassuring weight of the pack on your back confirms that your main parachute and reserve parachute—the most important part of the gear—are inside. Finally, you check your board, and then you are ready to go.

The side door of the airplane slides open for you and the **camera flyer**. As he adjusts the digital camera attached to his helmet, you pull your helmet on and secure the straps holding you on to your board. You have practiced these movements so many times and gone on so many jumps that all of the equipment feels like a familiar old friend. Finally, you pull on your webbed gloves.

The green light flashes, and the camera flyer gives you the thumbs-up sign. No matter how often you

A SKYSURFER AND HER CAMERA FLYER PREPARE TO LEAP INTO THE SKY.

have skysurfed, the jump never loses its thrill. Your heart is beating rapidly, and there are goose bumps up and down your arms.

With this rush of adrenalin, you are out the door. It feels like falling until your board catches that first blast of air. And then you're floating. Surfing the sky is like surfing the most radical set of ocean waves. Using your arms to guide you, you flip and turn, spin and twist, jump, loop around, and even somersault. You tip the board to the left and then to the right.

FLYING IN FORMATION

IF YOU LOVE the idea of skysurfing but are not quite up to it yet, you might want to try flying in formation, or what skydivers refer to as relative work (RW). Instead of jumping alone, you are a member of a team of jumpers, who, as they race to the earth below, assume the belly-to-earth position and join up in midair. By holding on to each other's wrists or to special grips sewn into the jumpsuits, the jumpers create a colorful pattern in the sky. One of the most popular formations is the star. Others include a red, white, and blue flag and a spiral. For formation fliers who are competing, the goal is to make as many different shapes as possible within the allotted time limit. Many teams compete to see how many jumpers they can get into a formation. In 2006 four hundred skydivers in Thailand held on to each other for just over four seconds; as of 2012, they held the record.

A new twist on free-fall-formation flying is canopy-formation skydiving, known to experts as CReW. Jumpers leave the plane one at a time and immediately open their parachutes. Joining up with their team members in the air, they link everything from their parachutes, suits, and parachute lines. Their patterns are typically built vertically instead of horizontally. As of 2012, the CReW world record was one hundred skydivers; it was set at the Florida Skydiving Center in Lake Wells, Florida, in 2007.

Another variation of skydiving that is growing in popularity is free flying, also known as vertical relative work (VRW). This style allows jumpers to get more creative. Falling positions include head-to-earth (head down), feet-to-earth (stand), back-to-earth (back flying), and seated (sit flying). Instead of staying either horizontal or vertical, as in the other styles, free-flying jumpers can do both and create a three-dimensional formation in the sky. As of 2012, the record for this type of flying was 108 jumpers, set in 2009 at Skydive Chicago.

THIS SKYSURFER TURNS SOMERSAULTS AS HE DESCENDS TO THE EARTH.

You surf the wind currents and cover great distances at high speed.

A MINUTE OF FREE FALL

For sixty glorious seconds you free-fall through space. Skysurfers experience multiple dimensions in a way that no other sport can offer. You can go left and right and forward and backward—as well as faster or slower. Professional free-fallers from the Dropzone website say, "Not even the NASA astronauts get to play in four dimensions." People who enjoy skysurfing compare it to a mix of sports; it combines the speed of auto racing, the precision of gymnastics, and the emotional rush of bungee jumping.

As good as it is, the thrill lasts for only one minute. Then it is time to prepare for landing. First, you grab a small handle that is attached to your pilot parachute. The handle pulls the chute out of its spot in the bottom of the parachute container and tosses it into the airstream. As the chute catches the air, it

THIS SKYSURFER SEEMS TO BE FLOATING ON AIR.

A SKYSURFER'S MAIN PARACHUTE OPENS AFTER THE PILOT CHUTE.

tugs on and releases the closing pin. This pin is what has held the main parachute container closed up until now. Once the pin is released, the main parachute is dragged out of the pack. It fills with air and slows your **descent**.

When you are just a few hundred feet off the ground, you pull the release that loosens the **bindings** around your feet. Your board dangles from your toes until just before you touch down. You curl your toes as you prepare to land, and the board drops safely to the ground nearby, followed in seconds by your body. Your skysurf has been a success.

TWO

TIME TO CATCH
A CLOUD

WHO CAME UP with the idea of jumping out of an airplane with a surfboard? Gary Patmor, a professional skydiver and aerospace engineer, claimed to be the first. His first effort, in 1965, failed, however; when he jumped out of a plane with a surfboard, it broke. For his next attempt he covered a surfboard with a coating of glue and glass to make it more durable. The board survived—and so did he. In 1980 a couple of other skydivers from California also decided to make skydiving a little more exciting; they tried jumping out of a plane while lying down flat on Styrofoam® boogie boards. Although they survived, the idea didn't catch on.

Over the next ten years, other jumpers followed these Californians' example. In 1986 two French skydivers, Dominique Jacquet and Jean-Pascal Oron, tried jumping with Styrofoam® boards again. They called it air surfing. A year later, a Frenchman named Joel Cruciani jumped with a surfboard strapped to his feet with snowboard bindings for a stunt in the film *Hibernator*. He was the first to stand up on one of these boards. Two years later, another Frenchman, Laurent Bouquet, jumped from a plane with a small, skateboardlike device on his feet.

WELCOME TO THE UNITED STATES

It was 1990 before the idea—and the name—of skysurfing started to be known in the United States. A jumper named Jerry Loftis helped make the sport famous. Besides participating in a number of competitions, he appeared on national television shows, in a music video, and in several television commercials.

14

He helped launch the World Freestyle Championships, the first to feature skysurfers. Loftis also created his own skysurfing company, Surflite, which specialized in making skysurfing-board accessories for jumpers. In addition, he developed lightweight boards, as well as a training system that showed student skysurfers how to work their way up from shorter boards to the more advanced longer boards. In 1998 Loftis died during a "fun jump." His main parachute malfunctioned on deployment, and he was unable to deploy his reserve chute in time.

In 1990 Patrick de Gayardon and Wendy Smith of New Zealand carried out the first tandem skysurf for a French sports film. They not only jumped together, but also skysurfed on the same board. Soon afterward,

PATRICK DE GAYARDON WAS WORLD RENOWNED FOR HIS DARING SKYDIVES.

they starred in several Japanese and European television commercials.

It was not until the following year, however, that most Americans saw skysurfing, when de Gayardon was featured in a Reebok commercial that told watchers, "Life is short. Play hard." People of all ages were fascinated by this exotic sport that took place up in the clouds. Several other commercials featuring skysurfers followed. In April 1993 the first skysurfing competition was held in Eloy, Arizona. Soon other competitions were held in California and Illinois. During the opening ceremonies of the 1994 Winter Olympics in Lillehammer, Norway, a four-man skysurfing team amazed the crowd with **aerial** acrobatics. The fascination with the sport continued to climb.

That same year, a skysurfer named Rob Harris and his camera flyer, Joe Jennings, won the second annual Skysurfing World Championships. Their victory was a surprise, as they were up against the team of de Gayardon and his camera flyer, Gus Wing, the previous year's winners. In 1995 Harris and Jennings

A SKYSURFER TAKES A JUMP DURING THE X GAMES IN OCEANSIDE, CALIFORNIA.

earned Entertainment and Sports Programming Network's (ESPN) Extreme Games (later the **X Games**) gold medal. They were definitely skysurfing's world champions. Harris grabbed the attention of viewers all over the world when he appeared skysurfing in a number of commercials. In 1998 de Gayardon died during a jump in Hawaii when he was testing an experimental wing suit.

COMMERCIAL TIME

ONE OF THE best ways to spread the word about a new idea is through television—especially commercials. A number of skysurfers, including Troy Hartman, the 1997 X Games gold medalist, have been featured in ads. In a soft-drink commercial aired during the 1998 Super Bowl, Hartman, shown catapulting through the air on his board, is joined by a daring goose who imitates his every move. The two exchange a few moves, take a long drink of soda, and then wave goodbye to each other. Hartman's quick moves were filmed by Joe Jennings, his camera flyer.

Meeting the Camera Flyer

As interest in the sport of skysurfing began to spread throughout the world, more and more competitions were set up. With all of the moves and tricks performed thousands of feet up in the air, how could the aerial acrobatics of the skysurfers possibly be judged?

The answer to that question is what makes skysurfing competition so challenging. Not only does a skysurfer have to be able to twist, turn, spin, jump, loop, and somersault through the air, but a partner, known as the camera flyer (whose helmet has a digital camera mounted on it), has to jump out of the plane, too. The camera flyer has to know where to point the camera in order to keep the jumper in sight and capture his or hers skilled moves. The camera flyer, therefore, must be a great jumper, too, as well as being comfortable with getting great shots while plummeting toward the earth at speeds of up to 180 miles per hour (290 kilometers per hour). In addition, he has to match the **fall rate** of the skysurfer—one of the trickiest parts of the job. The jumper and camera

A DIGITAL CAMERA IS MOUNTED TO A CAMERA FLYER'S HELMET.

flyer must move in unison to get the best shots of the action. Since the jumper often shifts from fast to slow, depending on which tricks and moves are being done, keeping pace can be challenging.

In the X Games, the camera on the camera flyer's helmet sends a live feed to the judges down on the ground so that they can watch and score the skysurfer's performance. In other competitions, the camera flyer's video is watched and judged once the team has returned to the ground.

The role of the camera flyer is so important that often the jump is judged as a team sport, with both participants' skills taken into account. Typically, the

A CAMERA FLYER VIDEOS A SKYSURFER DURING THE BOARDS OVER EUROPE COMPETITION IN SWITZERLAND.

jumpers are scored on technical ability and artistic merit. At the end of sixty seconds, both the jumper and the camera flyer have to prepare to land.

By 2000 skysurfing was a hot sport. People watched the sport in soft-drink commercials on television as well as at international competitions. Few could have predicted that in 2001 skysurfing would be dropped from the roster of the X Games— or that, over the years, so many of the pioneers of the sport would be lost to a variety of skydiving accidents. Nevertheless, some of the best jumpers continue to work to keep the sport alive and hold out hope that one day it will be back in the X Games and in the attention of sports lovers everywhere.

THREE

GEAR UP

RIDING THE SKY thousands of feet up in the air takes guts, determination, and skill. It also requires a great deal of jumping experience.

The schools that teach jumpers to skysurf often require at least two hundred regular skydiving jumps before they will accept a student. Some require at least one thousand jumps. As a professional jumper named Stefan Klaus said, "You can't learn skysurfing in two or three weeks. If you want a hobby, choose free flying. For skysurfing, you need at least eight hundred jumps until you can control the board the way you want it." Some dive-training centers expect

23

SKYDIVING IS A PREREQUISITE TO SKYSURFING. LESSONS ARE A MUST, AS WELL AS MANY SINGLE AND GROUP JUMPS.

new students to have experience with group free falls before enrolling.

A special license may be required. In the United States skydiving is governed by the **Federal Aviation Administration (FAA)**, as well as by the United States Parachute Association. Some states only require a Class A, or basic, license. To earn one of these you need to have completed twenty-five jumps, as well as five group skydives. Many **drop zones**, however, have higher requirements. They state that jumpers must have a B (expert), C, (advanced), or D (master) license in order to skysurf. B licenses require fifty jumps completed, plus the ability to land on a target or in water and perform a variety of basic aerial tricks. A C license indicates that a surfer has completed two hundred jumps and can perform complicated aerial maneuvers. The master, or Class D, license is given to those who complete five hundred or more jumps, plus participate in night jumps alone and with a group.

Another thing a skysurfer needs is equipment. The list is short and simple—but what there is can be quite expensive. Basic skysurfing equipment includes a strong helmet, which can cost $40 and up. The two parachutes are quite a bit more expensive: a primary parachute can run as much as $2,000, and the reserve chute can run half as much.

Skysurfing parachutes are somewhat different from those used by traditional skydivers. Instead of opening quickly when they are **deployed**, main canopies open gradually to allow for a more gentle descent. The reserve parachute, on the other hand, opens much more quickly. To ensure that it is functional and safe, it should be opened every six months and inspected by an expert. Some jumpers attach a computer on both the main and the reserve chutes. The computer, called an automatic activation device (AAD), is designed to gauge the air pressure of the surrounding area. If it detects a certain preset **altitude** and the surfer has not yet opened the chute, the computer sends a signal to the chute to open automatically.

Another important piece of equipment, the harness, can cost as much as $2,000. Some surfers like to wear webbed gloves, which, because they have no gaps between the fingers, give more control and make it possible to start and stop spins more quickly. The form-fitting Lycra suits that most surfers wear create less drag in the air. There is no need for special shoes; skysurfers typically wear laced-up running shoes. Most jumpers carry an **altimeter**, an instrument for measuring altitude. These start at about $150. For additional safety, some skysurfers also carry an audible altimeter, which is mounted on

THIS SKYSURFER HAS THE PROPER EQUIPMENT, SUCH AS A HARNESS, A HELMET, AND GLOVES.

the helmet. These devices are about $200 and are designed to beep at preset altitudes so that the jumper always knows how far it is to the ground.

Because of the expense of these items, many skysurfers buy used equipment to save money. It is essential that every piece of used gear be inspected by an FAA-licensed parachute rigger to guarantee that it is safe and secure.

MANY SKYSURFERS WEAR AN ALTIMETER WHEN THEY JUMP. IT MEASURES ALTITUDE.

LEARNING THE LINGO

IF YOU WANT to talk about skysurfing, you have to make sure you can speak the language. Here are some terms you might hear flying around between jumpers:

BOOGIE a special gathering of skysurfers for an event, often involving jumping from exotic aircraft such as helicopters, hot-air balloons, and biplanes

CANOPY a parachute

CUT AWAY to release the main parachute

DECISION ALTITUDE the altitude at which a jumper is trained to start emergency procedures

DROP ZONE a skydiving center

FLARE to put on the brake of the chute to slow its descent

RIG the entire parachute

RIGGER a person who packs, inspects, and repairs parachutes

Buying the Board

In skysurfing one of the most important purchases is the board. Prices usually run between $300 and $1,300. The board comes in a variety of sizes, and which one you choose depends on your skill level, as well as your height and weight. Although most boards are between 10.5 and 11 (26 and 27 centimeters) inches in width, the length may vary from a beginner's board of 32 inches to the longest one at 60 inches (81 cm to 152 cm).

THE MOST IMPORTANT PIECE OF EQUIPMENT IS THE BOARD.

Despite the difference in length, all of the boards tend to be quite light, weighing less than 5 pounds. The newest ones are made out of carbon graphite and **fiberglass**. They have a honeycomb core made out of aluminum. Along with size differences, most boards also come with a variety of shoe bindings, graphics, and decals.

After the equipment and the lessons are paid for, there are still the expenses of the air time in the plane, the gas, and the pilot's time. Prices vary greatly, but the average flight tends to cost the jumper around $75.

Although skysurfing requires a good deal of money for training and equipment, most jumpers feel that the thrill and excitement from each jump more than makes up for the cost.

IN ORDER TO SKYSURF, YOU NEED TO PAY FOR THE PLANE, PILOT, AND GAS.

FOUR

RIDING THE WIND

WHAT QUALITIES MAKE an accomplished skysurfer? Many of the skills required are the same ones you need to develop when you first learn to skydive. Clearly, you cannot be afraid of heights. Jumping out of an airplane should be exciting, not frightening. You have to be able to figure out your altitude and know when to pull the lever for your pilot chute. In addition, you must be physically fit because sky surfing takes endurance and muscle power.

Spending time watching videos of skysurfers is a great way to become familiar with the sport. Videos are available on the Internet, as well as from public

RIDING THE WIND REQUIRES BALANCE AND AGILITY.

libraries, mail-order catalogs, and specialty-gear shops. Watching these videos is an excellent way to see how tricks are done—and how to get out of trouble should it occur.

It is easy to see what skills are needed for the sport when you watch skysurfers perform. A strong sense of balance, for example, is essential. Next is agility; you have to get back on top of the board if you happen to lose control in the air. Typically, this move, often called recovery, is done by getting into a basic belly-to-earth position. Once that position is achieved, the skysurfer gets the board back underneath him or her by doing a front flip into a standing position.

Working with the Wind

The wind is the skysurfer's blessing—and curse. It is what gives the rider the ability to move from one place to another to make the turns, twists, and tricks. On the other hand, wind can also be dangerous. If the wind meets the board at the wrong angle, for example, it can create an unwanted spinning action.

WIND CURRENTS ALLOW SKYSURFERS TO PERFORM TRICKS AND MOVES IN DIFFERENT DIRECTIONS.

If a skysurfer loses control on the board, he might find himself in a side (or flat) spin. When this happens, the skysurfer is in a horizontal position, with the board out to the side. This type of spin can cause such confusion and dizziness for the rider that it is very difficult to slow it down. If the spin accelerates, within a matter of seconds, the blood rushing to the surfer's head will cause a loss of consciousness.

What happens to a rider who is in the middle of an out-of-control sidespin? The first step is knowing how to stop a spin and get back into the standing position. Although some teachers suggest that the surfer pull the release handle on the board in order for the skyboard to separate and bring the spin to an end, most experts believe this maneuver should be used only as a last resort. In order to do this cutaway move, the board release handle, which is worn on the upper thigh, has to be pulled. The handle connects to a long cable that is snaked up the surfer's pant leg. Once pulled, the cable releases the foot bindings, and the jumper and the board are immediately separated.

One of the first moves that new skysurfers learn is simply standing upright and keeping the nose of the board tipped downward. This movement in the air creates a forward motion known as tracking. It can be powerful and fast when it works right, but it can also, if not done quite right, cause the surfer to flip over. It takes a great deal of practice to master.

The beginning skysurfer rides with his feet turned sideways on the board, as when riding a snowboard. This position allows him to deploy from the basic belly-to-earth position. As the rider improves, he can deploy from a standing position instead, by changing the position of his feet so that one is behind the other, as when slalom waterskiing.

Given the extremely short time a skysurfer has to do his stunts (one minute) and the dangers of falling and riding on a board at the same time, the main trick is often just being able to stay upright and move from one spot to another. Skysurfing is such an extreme sport that just completing a dive is considered success.

THE BASIC MOVE OF SKYSURFING IS TO STAND
UPRIGHT ON THE BOARD AND TIP THE NOSE IN
A DOWNWARD POSITION.

BASE JUMPING

IF YOU LIKE jumping through space and want to take an even bigger risk than skysurfing, you could try BASE jumping. BASE stands for building, antenna, span, and earth. BASE jumpers do not leap from planes. They jump from stationary places such as bridges, buildings, waterfalls, cliffs, mountains, and other natural precipices. They have special chutes designed to deploy quickly.

The biggest annual gathering of BASE jumpers in the United States takes place at the New River Gorge Bridge in Fayette County, West Virginia. This event began in 1979 and has been held the third weekend of October each year since. During the Bridge Day Festival, more than eight hundred jumpers get together to jump from the bridge into the gorge below. Crowds exceeding 200,000 come to watch. BASE jumping is also allowed year-round from the Perrine Bridge in Twin Falls, Idaho, and during the annual Go Fast Games at the Royal Gorge Bridge in Cañon City, Colorado.

The sky has been a playground for many daring athletes. It invites people to come and play. Skysurfers are a brave bunch of people who are thrilled to spend a minute spinning and turning, flipping and flying, and, just for a moment, ignoring the gravity that is pulling at their feet. Although it is undoubtedly a dangerous sport designed for the most adventurous spirits, skysurfing is a thrill that has no match.

GLOSSARY

aerial of, in, or produced by the air

altimeter an instrument that indicates altitude

altitude the height of an object or point relative to
sea level

bindings the straps that hold a skysurfer's feet to
the board

camera flyer a person who shoots skydiving and
skysurfing video

deploy to spread out or get in a position for
a purpose

descent the act or process of moving downward,
dropping, or falling

drop zones skydiving centers

Federal Aviation Administration (FAA) the U.S.
agency that regulates flight-related activities

fall rate the rate at which a skysurfer or
skydiver descends

fiberglass a reinforced plastic material composed of
glass fibers embedded in resin

formation a group of skydivers forming a particular pattern while gripping each other's arms and legs

free flying skydiving in the bell-to-earth, feet first, or head first positions

harness a piece of gear with straps that secure equipment, such as a parachute pack, to a skysurfer

X Games an annual competition featuring extreme-action sports

FIND OUT MORE

BOOKS

Gigliotti, Jim. *Skydiving*. North Mankato, MN: Child's World, 2011.

McFee, Shane. *Skydiving*. New York: PowerKids Press, 2008.

Young, Jeff. *Pulling the Rip Cord: Skydiving*. Minneapolis, MN: Checkerboard Books, 2011.

WEBSITES

Dropzone

www.dropzone.com

A website dedicated to skydiving; it includes forums, videos, and information about gear.

Parachutist

http://parachutistonline.com/

Parachutist, a newsmagazine from the United States Parachute Association, features articles, interviews, and columns about all types of parachuting sports.

Skydive World

www.skydiveworld.com/english/skysurfing.html

A site that includes links to resources, books, and educational videos on how to be a skysurfer.

INDEX

Page numbers in **boldface** are illustrations.

ABOUT THE AUTHOR

TAMRA B. ORR is the author of more than three hundred books for readers of all ages. A graduate of Ball State University with a degree in secondary education and English, Orr has written thousands of questions for national and state assessments. She lives in the Pacific Northwest with her dog, cat, husband, and three teenagers. In her fourteen spare minutes each day, she loves to read, write letters, and travel around the state of Oregon, while marveling at the breathtaking scenery.